MW01267865

The Church, What Is It?

Tom Spencer

WINEPRESS WP PUBLISHING

The Church, What Is It?
Copyright © 1998 by Tom Spencer
All rights reserved. No part of this publication may be reproduced, stored
in a retrieval system, or transmitted in any way by any means, electronic,
mechanical, photocopy, recording or otherwise, without the prior permis-
sion of the publisher, except for brief quotations in critical reviews or ar-
ticles, or as provided by USA copyright law.

Published by WinePress Publishing, PO Box 1406, Mukilteo, Wa 98275.

Unless otherwise indicated, all scripture quotations are from the The Holy
Bible: New International Version, copyright © 1978 by the New York International Bible Society.

Printed in the United States of America
ISBN 1-57921-116-X

Dedication

The Church is simply a reflection of Jesus in our lives, and because of that ageless truth, I am honored to dedicate this book to my wife Roanna, our children Marci and Aaron, and to our faithful friends who have allowed us to make mistakes.

What About Tom and Roanna Spencer?

After twenty years of digging, Roanna and I tapped into the main stream of the river of God. We have been digging, drilling, pushing our roots down, but once we finally hit water I felt two powerful conflicting emotions; sorrow and joy.

I was a young boy of 15, in the Midwest, with great dreams of life and fears of death, when I heard the message of eternal life, by accepting Jesus as my Savior and my Lord. I embraced the message and found a relationship with God through Jesus and His Word. After six months of this new life, I felt compelled to know more. Not just an urge, a zeal overcame me, like a treasure hunter or one with gold fever. I experienced a new dimension of life and an inner strength, that I now know as the power of the Holy Spirit, or the power of the Spirit of God.

About the same time, a girl named Roanna was experiencing identical life changes on the East Coast. After spending three years with the best teachers our areas had to offer, and digging as deep as we could with the tools available, we both met at a college where we wanted to be equipped to dig deeper into the things of God. After two years we studied about men and women who did hit the waters of God, but the latest well had dried up some sixty years before. Then it seemed that our teachers just showed us how to move sand around. I was frustrated but not stopped, because I heard the voice of the Spirit say, *dig, dig, dig!* I just didn't know where.

I could not accept that what I was experiencing in God was all that there was. I knew there was an underground river that was the source of all that we could see above. Roanna and I searched for older ones who had already started digging and tried to team-up with them. As we did, we discovered one of two things; either they got fearful of our fresh zeal, or we realized they strayed from their original goal of wanting the powerful presence of God, and settled for making a business out of digging. After trying to join with five different teams, the Spirit of God confirmed that we needed to see the pitfalls that each of these teams fell into, before He could show us where to dig. I still didn't realize the cost of a digging expedition like this, but I was about to find out.

We started getting closer to the mainstream a couple of years ago, when we were asked to make some of the greatest sacrifices yet. We had to drop off baggage that was keeping us from breaking through. We were not only fired from the last expedition, we lost our digging partners.

We were branded as outcasts, extremist, and unconventional diggers. The Spirit of God showed us the only way to fit through the tunnel we had dug was to leave all of our natural supplies and resources behind for this last leg of the dig. It was like the captain of a sailing vessel, who knows he has passed the point of no return. From this point on we were committed to enter into the presence of God or die. Hallelujah!

We were so close, the sand and dirt turned into mud, and we could smell water. But I turned and realized I lost my wife. Exhausted from the accusations, misplaced trust and loyalty, abused by previous taskmasters with their manipulation and secret agendas, she couldn't make it. I looked into her face and nothing was left except a faint distant stare. "My God I had killed my wife!" It was dark and quiet in that tunnel, as I lay there with my only friend on earth, nothing but a hollowshell in the cold wet mud. I felt all alone. That is, until I looked down the tunnel where we had come and there were people, just a handful, but never the less they were following. Then I heard the words of the Spirit of God saying, *Keep Digging!* I know the meaning of the scripture; in my weakness He is made strong, because it wasn't my natural strength that broke through that last wall, it was supernatural.

When the first gush of water came through it wasn't what many would expect. It came violently, carrying all kinds of tunnel debris. It was neither clear nor peaceful, it came with an overwhelming force. Some of those behind me screamed that I had tapped into the devil's camp, as they looked back and were swept away by the current. All I could do was to hang on to my wife, face this new presence head-on, and receive this incredible cleansing. I knew this was what we had been digging for.

After a time it seemed as if the worst was over and I opened my eyes, even though a little blurry I could see that we had tapped into the mainstream. The song in my heart was *God forgive me for I have made you to small in my eyes.* Little by little I realize that I am not ankle deep or knee deep, I am immersed in the river of God. Things look so different from this perspective. I looked behind me and there were some that made it. They too got to experience the breakthrough, some laughing, some choking and all of us overwhelmed. Then I turned to my wife and my hope had come to pass; new color in her face, she's breathing again, and her heart is full of life. Like the first flower that blooms in the Spring. She is alive! Truly, the same power that raised Christ from the dead shall quicken our mortal bodies.

We are no longer seasonally dependent on the few showers that would come and revive us in the desert. We have been transplanted by the River of Life with our roots going deep into the very source of life. Therefore, as our tree grows strong and tall, it bears fruit every month to nourish those around us and our leaves are like medicine to the sick.

The Church
What is it?

Every week thousands of gifts to the body of Christ are sitting at home, confused, hurt, isolated and unassembled. The gifts know that they love Jesus, but have had a hard time understanding what has been called the "Church." Most of these gifts have walked with Jesus for many years, and have desperately tried to "fit in" by "doing" everything that was expected of them. They have served many departments, given of their time and resources, and sat through endless hours of board meetings trying to help the Leader in his many decisions. But something was wrong, something was lacking and there seemed to be no solution, so they just quietly slipped home and never returned.

My purpose in writing this book is to give hope to those valuable gifts at home. It not only illustrates why some of the most lovable leaders in our churches can be caught in an ugly trap, but it also gives a picture of Jesus' church, which is alive and well today! Even in the sorry condition of the seven churches of Asia Jesus still referred to them as golden *"...and the seven (golden) lamp stands are the seven churches"* (Rev. 1:20). Listen, Jesus gave his very life for the church and He still considers them valuable containers of His presence!

9

However, if a sailing ship was traveling from Cordova Alaska to San Francisco, California, and its navigation was one degree off, eventually it would wind up in Chile, South America.

Jesus only mentioned the word church twice in all of his teachings, do you suppose what we have today was what He intended? Or could it be that the church got one degree off 1500 years ago, and has not only not hit the bulls eye, but has missed the target altogether? Do we dare ask this question?

This book is by no means a complete exhaustive theological study on the subject of The Church. But I do believe by understanding the history, it might help you see a bigger picture and if you are sitting home, this might answer some of your questions.

I too have been wounded by what has been called the "Church", and some of my writing reflects those scars. My intent is not to throw stones but to reveal my process. I pray that you find it as life changing as I did.

Tom Spencer

Introduction

Apostle Paul warned us 1900 years ago that a foundation had been laid of which to build the church but to be careful how we build on it (I Cor. 3:10-12).

Several years ago I listened to a tape of a Teacher in the body of Christ that was sharing his confession worldwide. He had built a large and strong organization with books, tapes, television and conventions but God revealed to him out of (I Cor. 3:13-15) that at the end of this mans life he was going to turn around and see his entire ministry judged by fire. He would see everything he built, burnt down and all of his life energy was of no heavenly value. Why? Because he was not careful how he built upon the foundation already laid.

This man was one of a few I know that heeded the warning and reduced his ministry to one third its size and stayed focused on the *"...gold, silver, and costly stones"* (I Cor. 3:12) that God had directed him in.

In the same way I took a hard look at what we were doing. This led me to start praying prayers like: *Lord, show me Your ways, make my crooked paths straight, cleanse me by Your presence, the washing of your Word, and the burning coal on your alter.* Wow! Here is what took place after six months of praying those prayers:

In September 1993, my wife and I facilitated a small study group every week in our home. The topic was, "What is the church?" Our goal was to understand and experience God's purpose, plan, structure and look for the church He had in mind. Our first approach was not to compare or use any example of a "church" that we had seen or been involved with. Instead we used only the Bible and the leading of the Holy

Spirit as our source. For several months we studied the only two times Jesus used the word "church" (Matt. 16:18 and 18:17).

We discovered several insights to the awesome authority of the church in relationships, but realized that there was no way that the traditional church system we had been submersed in for the past 20 years could begin to facilitate this authority and freedom. Why not? Because of the lack of true relationships. Thus, we broke our own rule of "no comparisons," so we flipped the question to ask, what is the Church *not?*

What the Church is Not

• The Church is not a building: Yet we have been deceived into believing it is. Why do we say, "Let's go to Church?"

• The Church is not a corporation: Even though our government encourages the body of Christ to register as a non-profit corporation with enticing tax breaks for financial donations.

• The Church is not a system of do's and don'ts, rules and regulations or programs and entertainment: Yet people have given many hours of their lives to writing rules, filling out requisitions, working to top last year's Christmas concert, and performing with perfection.

The Mystery Unfolds

Paul wrote in Eph. 5:32 that the church and Christ have been a profound mystery. *"No eye has seen, no ear has heard, no mind has conceived what God has prepared for those who love Him- but God has revealed it to us by His Spirit"* (1 Cor. 2:9,10). *"We have not received the spirit of the world but the Spirit who is from God that we may understand what God has freely given us"* (1 Cor. 2:12). Peter replied, *"Repent and be baptized, every one of you, in the Name of Jesus Christ for the forgiveness of your sins..."* (Acts 2:38). *"Those who accepted his message were baptized, and about three thousand were added to their number [the church] that day. They devoted themselves to the apostles' teaching and to the fellowship, to the breaking of bread, and to prayer"* (Acts 2:41-42). *"Everyday they continued to meet in the temple courts. They broke bread in their homes and ate together with glad and sincere hearts"* (Acts 2:46). *"Day after day in the temple courts and from house to house, they never stopped teaching and proclaiming the good news that Jesus is the Christ"* (Acts 5:42).

Turning Point—ACTS 8:1

Now take a look at what happened when Stephen, a disciple of Christ, was stoned to death. *"...On that day a great persecution broke out against the church at Jerusalem, and all except the apostles were scattered throughout Judea and Samaria. Godly men buried Stephen and mourned deeply for him. But Saul began to destroy the church. Going from house to house..."* Acts 8:1.

From this time on, we no longer see in scripture, the church meeting in temples. For some, history tells us, the "called out ones" were no longer accepted under the temple welfare system and were in fear of their lives. However, I'm sure that most had the revelation (at least in part) that Jesus opposed the temple system, and understood the kingdom of God was within them. This produced a whole new way of life, and the line had been drawn.

Even after Saul's conversion, we only see him (now known as Paul) and his ministry team entering the temples for debate and persuasion (Acts 13:14-42; 14:1; 17:2,10; 18:4,19). As Paul presented Jesus as the Messiah, some believed and came out of the temple-system and Paul raised them up to be leaders. They then started "ministry houses."

Our study group discovered a foundational truth on which to build—Acts 20:20.

"You know that I have not hesitated to preach anything that would be helpful to you but have taught you publicly and from house to house." Not temple to temple or synagogue to synagogue, but publicly [out in the open] and house to house" [in the intimacy of your homes] (Acts 20:20).

A New Beginning

It was at this point that everything we had practiced and taught concerning "the Church" was challenged.

We knew we were born again (Jn. 3:3, Rom.10:9,10) and we were not to be isolated individuals because the body needs each other (1 Cor. 12:12, Eph. 4:4). We also knew that Jesus was getting ready (getting us ready) to build His Church (Matt. 16:18) or in our case, tear down our old traditional concepts and start over. This was a time to tear down and start over (Ecc. 3:3). With God's help we let go, and threw out every preconceived idea and started over from the ground up.

We desired not to be people who just want to gripe about the traditional church system we came out of. We did not want a bunch of head knowledge to defend our victimized lives. But instead, we desired to be people who are trying to understand and experience God's will. We realized this was the point of no return. Jesus was asking for ALL of our old baggage to be dropped in order to fulfill our destiny in Him.

Every step of this transition was tremendously challenging. We had no idea how ingrained and attached we were to the traditional church system. As we still made some decisions according to the former way of doing things God would lovingly ask; Are you building the house or am I? Then through repentance and listening, God would give us direction that put us back on the main highway. God is the God of process!

Jesus is the Foundation

"For no one can lay any foundation other than the one already laid, which is Jesus Christ!" (1Cor. 3:11). *"...built on the foundation of the apostles and prophets, with Jesus Christ himself as the chief cornerstone"* (Eph. 2:20). *"For in Scripture it says: 'See, I lay a stone in Zion, a chosen and precious cornerstone, and the one who trusts in him will never be put to shame.'"* (1Pet. 2:6). (Further reference Isaiah 28:16.)

"So then, no more boasting about men" (1 Cor. 3:21). If we begin to highlight, praise, promote or advertise anything but Jesus, we have missed it. Even the Holy Spirit brings no attention to Himself. As we try to exalt The Holy Spirit He (The Spirit) always brings the attention back to the work and word of Jesus! *"But the Counselor, the Holy Spirit, whom the Father will send in my name, will teach you all things and will remind you of everything I (Jesus) have said to you"* (John 14:26).

Jesus is the Entrance

"I (Jesus) am the gate; whoever enters through me will be saved" (Jn. 10:9). *"I am the good shepherd; I know my sheep and my sheep know me"* (Jn. 11:14). Jesus does not *bring* life, salvation healing and resurrection. He *is* life, He *is* salvation, He *is* healing, He *is* resurrection (Jn. 11:25)! Jesus said, *"I am the way and the truth and the life. No one comes to the Father except through me"* (Jn. 14:6). *"...Because I live, you also will live"* (Jn. 14:19). Even John the Baptist, Jesus' forerunner said; *"He (Jesus) must become greater, I must become less"* (Jn. 3:30).

Jesus is the Building

"And in Him (Jesus) you too are being built together to become a dwelling in which God lives by His Spirit" (Eph. 2:22). *"...we will in all things grow up into Him who is the Head, that is, Christ"* (Eph. 4:15). *"...as Christ is the head of the church, His body, of which He is the Savior"* (Eph. 5:23). *"In Him the whole building is joined together and*

15

rises to become..." (Eph. 2:21) Jesus said *"I will build my church and the gates of hell will not overcome it."* (Matt. 16:18).

What is this building, temple, body, church that is being built up, growing up and joined together? What does it look like? How does it operate? What is its purpose?

The Subtle Deception

Question: What is this?

Answer: It's only a building.

Remember the rhyme we would do with our hands, "Here's the church, here's the steeple, open the door, and see all the people?"

It Was a Lie!

It doesn't matter if you gather in a beautiful stone building with stain glass windows or in a hotel meeting room; it is only a building. Even though it may have some great historical value or have great spiritual symbolism in the decor, it is still only a building constructed by the hands of men. It has no spiritual value. No building is Holy! It is God's *people* who bring His Holy Spirit into a place.

Buildings, Programs and Disappointments

So what's the big deal? Why the alarm? When we walk by a church building and our children say, "what a pretty church," or, "that church is big or small," a belief has been established that the building is the church. As that belief is used as a foundation of truth, and we build upon it, over time great disappointment and broken expectations begin to happen.

What about this one; "Daddy why do we have to spend so much time at church?" Can you see the setup for rebellion? We read the Bible and hear sermons that the gates of hell cannot prevail against "the church." If the church is a building, our spiritual war becomes a fight to save and defend a building and every system that supports that building. All kinds of resources; time, money and energy are spent on building "the church" building.

The precarious issue here is that if the building falls, the Church falls. Once "the church" building is built we don't know what to do with ourselves, so we develop programs inside "the church" (building) to keep the people busy. What do we call the programs? We call them "ministries."

New people (seekers) are drawn to "the church" building because of a youth ministry (program) or a music ministry (program), and it gets a little crowded in "the church" (building) so it's time to remodel, add a new wing or build a new building! And what about the leadership? They use their time spinning 20 ministry plates (programs) at a time, while playing additional roles of architect, realtor and general contractor. Does any of this sound familiar to you? Still you ask, "What's the big deal?" Let's continue.

First your sit through twelve weeks of a membership class and six weeks of a personal workers class, which are required to do any ministry (program) in "the church" (building). You then take additional training for the ministry (program) you feel called to: usher, parking lot, maintenance, nursery, children, Jr. high, Sr. high, college & career, singles 30 to 40, singles 40 to 50+, seniors, hospital, prison, Sr. homes, choir, drama, technical, home groups...shall I go on? After all of that process, one develops an expectation that they would be equipped to minister (Eph. 4:12). The promises and expectations would be:

- That one would have a deeper relationship with God
- A deeper relationship with each other
- A more powerful move of the Holy Spirit in one's life.

Instead, we find only around 10% of the congregation (usually the performance-based individuals) have the stamina or motive (good or bad) to complete such a rigorous course. After reaching the end of this great training, even they are disappointed because there is usually no deeper relationship with God.

Next, the disappointment that no great friendships came into being (i.e. lack of time, people checking children in with their teachers, then running to their own classes, or busy taking care of another ministry "program" item). There's just no time to talk. Plus, there is the hidden expectation of becoming friends with the established leaders, but because of political power struggles, friendships rarely happen. If by chance they do, the relationships don't last long.

What about a more powerful move of the Holy Spirit? That too takes a relationship, and this system is usually in too big of a hurry to wait and listen. One is trained to "make things happen" anyway. Oh, there is an appearance of relationships, as family seminars are taught, and certain testimonies are highlighted concerning friends, or advertisements are sent out like, **"The End of your Search for a Friendly Church."** But it doesn't take long to look closely and see that 10% are required to keep an image of relationships so that the other 90% of the people will do their job. If the image is not upheld, political power plays take place, and if not kept under wraps, there are new words introduced into our religious vocabulary, such as "church splits."

And the other 90%? Every performance needs an audience, and these 90% are expected to come to "the church" (building) once or twice a month, watch the performance, and give money to pay the bills. Where does it stop? Father, forgive us!

It is important that we see Satan's subtle lie that "the church" is a building. It is like building on sinking sand. When the rainstorm comes, no matter what we build, it will fall with great destruction. There's not even one temple building in the New Jerusalem (Rev. 21:22)!

The Mystery Revealed

Paul said the church and Christ have been a profound mystery (Eph. 5:32). *"No eye has seen, no ear has heard, no mind has conceived what God has prepared for those who love Him"* (Is. 64:4) *"...but God has revealed it to us by His Spirit"* (1 Co. 2:9,10). *"We have not received the spirit of the world but the Spirit who is from God that we may understand what God has freely given us"* (1Cor. 2:12).

The Church in its Smallest Form

Let's take a look at the smallest form of the church. Let me minister to you a personal word from the Lord on listening. *"He who has ears to hear let him hear what the Spirit has to say, be careful not to miss the most simple."*

Jesus said: *"Again, I tell you that if two of you on earth agree about anything you ask for it will be done for you by my Father in heaven. For where two or three come together in my name, there I am with them"* (Mt. 18:19,20). That means we are all meant to be ministers! Not just one to ten men or women who run an organization of sixty (the average "church" size in America) to three thousand people. If Jesus said it only takes two to get Him to show up and manifest His miracle working presence, then odds are, that one of those two is going to have to minister! Praise God!

We now understand that the church is not a building, but we must also realize it is not even a "place"! Even those following the "Cell" Church pattern or a "House to House" model, may start believing that the house is a Church. Jesus never intended his church to be a place where people come to. The church *is* people. We were never intended to be limited by giving or receiving ministry at a certain place or time.

Whenever two or more believers find themselves together or plan to meet, we have church going on! For example: two believers run into each other at the grocery store, one shares a need, the other takes the believer by the hand (no show, make it look like you are shaking hands, and stop yelling) and prays a prayer of agreement. This *is* Church! No waiting for Sunday or Wednesday, no limitation of going to a certain "Holy place." Jesus said we shall do greater things than Him (Jn. 14:12). Prayer is the greater thing (Jn. 14:13)! *"And the prayer offered in faith will make the sick person well; the Lord will raise him up. If ... sinned, he will be forgiven"* (James 5:15).

Spiritual House

"The kingdom of God is within you... " (Lk. 17:21). *"Do you not know that your body is a temple of the Holy Spirit, who is in you, whom you have received from God"* (1 Cor. 6:19)? *"...you also like living stones, are being built up into a spiritual house"* (1Pet. 2:5). After viewing the New Jerusalem, John said; *"I did not see a temple in the city, the Lord God Almighty and the Lamb are its temple"* (Rev. 21:22).

The expansion of the church was not done temple to temple but house to house. These home fellowships were led by Elders, and the Apostle Paul later addressed them as the church in Colossi, Ephesus, etc. From Acts 8:1 we no longer see in scripture the church meeting in temples (buildings). We see relationships thriving together under the Headship of Jesus, and with the demonstration of the power of the Holy Spirit (1 Cor. 2:1)!

"They broke bread in their homes and ate together with glad and sincere hearts, praising God and enjoying the favor of all the people. And the Lord added to their number daily those who were being saved" (Acts 2:46-47). *"All the believers were one in heart and mind. No one claimed that any of his possessions was his own, but they shared everything they had"* (Acts 4:32). *"There were no needy persons among them. For from time to time those who owned land(s) or house(s) sold them, brought the money from the sales and put it at the apostles' feet; and it was distributed to anyone as he had need"* (Acts 4:34,35). In Gal. 5:1, Paul was writing to people about circumcision in particular, but freedom from the law as a whole (of which temple worship is a major part) states; *"Stand fast therefore in the liberty where with Christ hath made us free, and be not entangled again with the yoke of bondage"* (KJV).

Again we asked ourselves the same questions you are pondering, "Lord, do I dare to believe this? Did you really intend it to be this easy?" I will show you the complete picture of "the structure" at the end of this book, but at this point we asked a couple of important facilitating questions. (1) If this is the simplicity of the church, then why don't we see the "ministers" promoting it? (2) Why wouldn't everyone jump at the chance to be equipped to do the work of the ministry?

Buckle your seat belt, because from here on it gets a little rocky.

Love of Money, Pride & Image

What is the force behind every sin? Every murder, sex crime, drug deal, computer tap, or theft has the same root—love of money.

"If anyone teaches false doctrines and does not agree to the sound instruction of our Lord Jesus Christ and to godly teaching, he is conceited and understands nothing. He has an unhealthy interest in controversies and quarrels about words that result in envy, strife, malicious talk, evil suspicions and constant friction between men of corrupt mind, who have been robbed of the truth and who think that godliness is a means to financial gain.

"But godliness with contentment is great gain. For we brought nothing into the world, and we can take nothing out of it. But if we have food and clothing, we will be content with that. People who want to get rich fall into temptation and a trap and into many foolish and harmful desires that plunge men into ruin and destruction."

"For the love of money is the root of all evil..." 1 Tim. 6:3-10 (KJV).

Most ministers working in the traditional church system are caught in a trap. They were called and anointed by God, but chose perhaps the only route they could see which is pastoring a building ministry.

When a minister has the overhead of a corporate staff, real estate, programs, events, plus buildings and repairs, it takes money. I was in one "church" (building) where all office staff were asked to turn off our lights every time we walked out of our office, and it saved us $500 a month.

It takes money! Then the minister starts counting on a certain amount of "income" (tithes & offerings) coming in each month, thus determining the "church" building budget. Next yearly projections are made. He (the minister), then goes to the bank with his yearly "income" projections and gets a loan to build bigger and fancier facilities. An image begins to appear. The loan goes through, stress goes up, and the demands grow bigger. Thus the trap gets tighter. Grumbling is on the increase, and the offerings on a decrease, so here come the money sermons, with well known "evangelists" (heavy hitters) to shame the body into giving. Oh no! What if the weather turns cold and say a snowstorm hits. The minister blames it on the devil because people can't come to the "church" (building) and bring their money. Now the projected "offerings" (income) has not come in and interest payments can't be made. The minister's image is tarnished, and he is at a crossroads.

If you are a minister in a traditional church system church and this book has slipped into your hands, hear the Word of our Lord for you. You can't bind it, you can't loose it, you can't fix it. You can only come out from among it. (Rev. 18:4.)

It is important to understand that the minister is now caught in an ugly, evil trap. It is one of the top demonic temptations that attack leaders. Sex, money, power and pride! In the last twenty years I have never personally known a leader, when faced with the battle of his own pride, to ever conquer it while in this system. At this point they have believed the lie that they are in too deep now, and have to come up with a fleshly scheme to raise the needed income. This is where "marketing companies" have been hired to raise money by using Mark 4:20 to sell "Holy Dirt" from Jerusalem, or "Holy Water" from the Jordan River.

Again, the minister may not want to push this hard for money, but he is blind and caught in a trap. The latest heartbreaker I recently heard about was on a Sunday a leader demanded that 100 people come to the front of the sanctuary and put $1,000 each in the offering. He was pressured to do this to catch up on past church bills. This type of spiritual abuse is a downward spiral where both pastor and congregation lose. Do you get the picture? A pastor in this kind of a system couldn't encourage the idea of educating and training the body to minister freely in their homes, because the "income" would then plummet, and there would be no need for the created image.

Oh Father, forgive us and make our crooked paths straight.

All People Accountable to God

Which brings us to our second question. Why wouldn't every believer jump at the chance to be discipled and equipped to do the work of the ministry (Eph. 4:6)? Many believers have been trained to work 40-60 hours a week and pay "the professional clergy" to minister. The thought of being accountable to know the scripture and share it with someone else is almost unbearable. And what about having an intimate relationship with God?

Human nature says, "it is always easier to follow a set of rules than to actually have a relationship with the rule maker." Then push them over the edge and ask them to open their home once or twice a week for all kinds of people to come tromping through to be discipled. What? No "professional clergy" to serve communion, dedicate a baby, baptize in water, or cast out a demon? Most would say, *"Forget it! Let me stay in a safe, secure, building ministry. This freedom is too hard!"* Paul writes in Gal. 5:1, *"It is for freedom that Christ has set us free. Stand firm, then, and do not let yourselves be burdened again by a yoke of slavery."*

A Look at History

Constantine:

From Acts chapter eight, to the report of the Roman Emperor Constantine supposedly being saved, the church had been operating almost 400 years in its purest form—"house to house." During the Roman persecution, Christians were forced to the underground catacombs. Here historians have uncovered several chambers where 40-50 believers could squeeze in to worship God corporately. But, they didn't just go to church there, they lived there. The catacombs were their homes. They raised their children, ate, worshipped and buried their dead there.

The birth of the "Bride of Christ"—the Church—was delivered and sealed with great blood shed, and Satan's first plan was to destroy the Church with violence. Christians were tortured and greatly persecuted. However, the more that were killed, the more others would spring up and take their place.

Satan then changed his tactics. His next plan was to stop the persecution and substitute it with the allurements of temporal prosperity and worldly honor, which usually come with "building ministry."

Once Constantine, a so-called born again Roman Emperor, called off the feud against God's people, he opened up massive public buildings and gave them to the "Church." With a well thought out military plan, it took Satan only 400 years to gradually re-establish "temple worship".

Paul warned us not to allow this old leaven to enter because it would ruin the whole batch (1 Cor. 5:7). History shows us that eventually it did.

Paganism:

There was a catch to Constantine opening the public buildings. What it did was bring unity between two spiritual groups— Paganism and Christianity. He had the hope that the Christians would influence and win the pagans to Christ. But the result was disastrous, as the Christians lowered their standards through the many compromises.

History shows that the Pagans claimed to accept Christ and join the followers of Jesus, but they continued to worship idols. The only difference was that they changed the objects of their worship from statues of frogs, snakes, trees and dead ancestors to images of Jesus, Mary—and even the Apostles themselves.

Romanism:

This was a resurrection of the old legal system with a new look. Again this was a system of making buildings, statues, cups and clothes sacred, but added the focus of idol worship which came with the Pagan influence. This began an infiltration of lustful, greedy and power-hungry motives that not only took over the Roman Government, but also the body of Christ. The takeover happened by slowly removing the written word of God from the general public and promoting men (professional clergy, as keepers of the Scriptures). They were to be the only ones qualified to handle the Holy Scriptures. Thus we were led into the Dark Ages. Without the Word of God, superstitions ran wild and the general public began to believe anything.

Dark Ages:

Clergy set themselves up as God Himself, and purgatory was introduced to hold the public in fear. With the Doctrine of Indulgences, money began to exchange hands, where people could make payments to "the church" to get their dead loved ones out of the fire of purgatory and into heaven. Either Constantine was Satan himself parading as an "Angel of Light," a truly naive follower of Jesus, or was he just used of Satan as was Peter (Matt. 16:23)? History points to him as the one who re-established temple worship, professional clergy, and the one who encouraged Christians to come back into buildings. Whatever the answer is, he was certainly used to entangle again the once free body of Christ with the yoke of bondage (Gal. 5:1).

Martin Luther:

From the 4th century to the 16th century, this dark demonic system went along without challenge until a man named Martin Luther arrived on the scene. At the age of 18, Luther entered the University of Erfurt and discovered a Latin Bible, a book he had never seen before. Can you imagine? Luther, a believer and follower of Jesus, who didn't fit into this Romanism system, now armed with the Bible (1 Cor. 4), opposed the system. He used the Scriptures, the Truth, the Word of God, as his defense.

The Church Reformation:

Unfortunately, as time has revealed, we went from one ditch to the other. As Luther debated the unscriptural practices of the Church (named Romanism or Roman Catholicism) he met great political opposition. Luther was soon excommunicated and labeled the "devil in the flesh." Trying to follow the Word of God, Luther found himself leading a new system, which was eventually called *The Protestants*.

Those who followed Luther, the Protestants, would have done great had they just separated themselves and gone their way with God (Rev. 18:4 "come out from among them"). However, the ditch they fell into was to continue to fight and debate the Catholic system. Their war became the great task of proving their system right and converting Catholics to become Protestants. The very thing the Protestants hated and protested against, was the very thing they ended up with—even today.

The Roman Catholics had ultimate power and government control. They set up clergy to be as God, and didn't allow people freedom of the knowledge of The Word—let alone a personal relationship with Jesus Christ, the Son of God. People had to go through a priest in order to get to God. Because of a lack of knowledge (Hosea 4:6) the people were controlled, manipulated and abused by power-hungry men with evil demonic motives...these leaders were driven by greed, lust and pride.

Today the Protestant system looks different, but has ultimately become the same monster as Catholicism. It is similar to the independence of the United States and the government of democracy. The Protestants rule, control and manipulate through a democratic process called politics. Voting and the democratic process gives a feel of freedom of choice in their present system.

It doesn't always sound as ugly as this when power-hungry men and women position themselves to be rulers. As the love of money (1 Tim. 6:10) comes into play, they too become driven by lust, greed and pride. They find themselves manipulating people to achieve their own underlying agendas.

The minister's long flowing robes and white collar have been exchanged for a suit and tie. The beautiful stained glass windows with the ringing bell in the steeple is replaced with a seminar room at a nearby hotel. However, it is the same old system, the same old monster. We have now come out of one ditch and jumped straight into the other.

End of the Battle

It has been proven that Satan cannot extinguish the Word, the Spirit or the Church. But he can, and has, neutralized it. The enemy of the Church tries to get our eyes off the true commission, *"He said to them, Go into all the world and preach the good news to all creation. Whoever believes and is baptized will be saved, but whoever does not believe will be condemned. And these signs will accompany those who believe: In my name they will drive out demons; they will speak in new tongues; they will pick up snakes with their hands; and when they drink deadly poison, it will not hurt them at all; they will place their hands on sick people, and they will get well"* (Mark 16:15).

If Satan can keep us fighting in the flesh between other religious opinions he has neutralized, nullified—and won. *"Thus you nullify the word of God by your tradition that you have handed down..."* (Mark 7:13).

Scripture says to, *"Put on the full armor of God so that you can take your stand against the devil's schemes. For our struggle is not against flesh and blood, but against the rulers, against the authorities, against the powers of this dark world and against the spiritual forces of evil in the heavenly realms"* (Eph. 6:11,12). Still today these two religious groups spend much of their time and energy either fighting each other, or making a truce to join each other.

The end of the battle with these two large groups led by Satan is when they outwardly lay down their weapons and unite themselves (with other political forces) as one world power, or one-world order (Rev.18). Sound familiar? The union has been happening for some time, but we are just now seeing it become public.

What Does the Church Look Like if it is Not a Building?

Now that I have totally given modern day religion a "shake down" is there any hope at all for the church? Yes! Here is the fun part! We, as a small study group, and as a remnant in the body of Christ (Rev. 12:17), are not called to "fix" the old system. We have to start over. The Word doesn't tell us to fix, bind, loose, cast our or pray for that old system. We are commanded to come out from among it (Rev. 18:4). At this point I would like to minister to you a super injection of power and refreshing of God's Word!

"Follow peace ...and holiness" (Heb. 12:14*). "Say to wisdom, "You are my sister," and call understanding your kinsman;"* (Prov. 7:4). *"Surely goodness and love will follow me all the days of my life, and I will dwell in the house of the LORD forever"* (Psalm 23:6). *"If any of you lacks wisdom, he should ask God, who gives generously to all without finding fault, and it will be given to him. But when he asks, he must believe and not doubt..."* (James 1:5,6).

The Family—A Proven Working Model of the Church

In the book of Acts several things are taken for granted. The church was birthed at a certain time, in a certain culture with certain built-in features. One of the most important features was the relationship of family.

Jesus consequently used "family terms" to describe the Kingdom of God and the relationships involved. Let's watch as the family begins and the relationship enters; *"The virgin will be with child and will give birth to a son, and they will call him Immanuel"* —which means, *"God with us"* (Mat. 1:23). *"The Word became flesh and made his dwelling among us. We have seen his glory, the glory of the One and Only, who came from the Father, full of grace and truth"* (Jn.1:14). *"In my Father's house are many rooms;"* (Jn. 14:2). *"The younger one said to his father, 'Father, give me my share of the estate'"* (Lk. 15:12). *"Father, the time has come. Glorify your Son, that your Son may glorify you"* (Jn. 17:1). *"...that all of them may be one, Father, just as you are in me and I am in you. May they also be in us..."* (Jn. 17:21).

Paul made this bold statement using family terms; *"Even though you have ten thousand guardians in Christ, you do not have many fathers, for in Christ Jesus I became your father through the gospel. Therefore I urge you to imitate me"* (I Co. 4:15,16). And later wrote that; *"And you have forgotten that word of encouragement that addresses you as sons: 'My son, do not make light of the Lord's discipline, and do not lose heart when he rebukes you, because the Lord disciplines those he loves, and he punishes everyone he accepts as a son'"* (Heb. 12:5,6).

John continued the family theme when he described the development of a new Christian from a child to a mature father figure. *"I write to you, dear children... I write to you, fathers, ...I write to you, young men..."* (I Jn. 2:12,13).

Paul describes God's governmental order using the marriage; *"For the husband is the head of the wife as Christ is the head of the church, his body, of which he is the Savior... and gave himself up for her"* (Eph. 5:23-25). Show me a man that will give himself up for his wife, and I will show you a wife that will freely submit to his authority.

Now notice how God's governmental order continues in the same family principle; *"Children, obey your parents in the Lord, for this is right. 'Honor your father and mother—which is the first commandment with a promise—that it may go well with you and that you may enjoy long life on the earth.' Fathers, do not exasperate your children; instead, bring them up in the training and instruction of the Lord"* (Eph. 6:1-4).

It is so clear that God establishes His authority with the family chain of command through dependency and submission. A baby is dependent on the parents for all his provisions; food, shelter, clothing, love and education. A wife is dependent on her husband to be the leader, and final decision maker (personally accountable to God), in their home. *"...a man will leave his father and mother and be united to his wife"* (Eph. 5:31). A husband is totally dependent on God for life, guidance, wisdom and understanding. This chain of command is blessed if it is honored through serving and relationship. But if any part of this chain is broken through abuse of the authority or rebellion to the authority, our home seems to be dwelling in a living hell. Filled with violence, impure motives and a self-seeking existence, the blessing is removed.

"For rebellion is as the sin of witchcraft, and stubbornness is as iniquity and idolatry. Because thou hast rejected the word of the LORD, he hath also rejected thee from being king" (I Sam. 15:23 KJV). As we reject the authority of God, likewise our authority is removed. Rebellion says; "I won't do it." and stubbornness says; "I'll do it, but I will do it my way."

I know you are probably thinking that most homes in the United States, and around the world, are broken, dysfunctional, stubborn, rebellious, abused and violent places of existence where authority is a joke. Well, not in my home. And possibly not in your home either. We have to start somewhere. I have decided to embrace the will of God for my life and be the righteous man God wanted me to be. I made a decision to rule my household the way Christ rules the church; through loving sacrifice and authority. My wife and I are raising our children to honor and respect people and proper authority and that includes God and his government. You can do the same.

So when do we get to this proven working model of the church you promised? We have introduced half of it already. Did you miss it? It starts with the family. The church is wherever two or more believers are gathered together under Godly authority, and that begins with your family Praise God!

No Order without Government

The challenge comes when families start assembling together, which requires the next level of government. Now remember, just as all dads are not abusers, all ministers are not corrupt. Remember, that as all dads are to be a blessing to the family as men under authority, so all ministers are to be a blessing to the Body of Christ as they too are under authority.

According to scripture all dads are required to have the same moral and character qualifications but each is given the freedom to lead his family in the personality and style he chooses. In the same way, all ministers have the same moral and character qualifications but each has the freedom and flexibility to mold his ministry as he sees fit. Of course both parties use wisdom by asking for insight and counsel, but when the rubber meets the road that dad has to make some hard decisions for his family and answer to God for his choices. The minister also has to make tough decisions and answer to God for his choices.

The whole making- or breaking-point of a family or a church is based on this one factor of governmental authority. If we don't understand the purpose of something, it could bring (and has brought) great harm. The purpose of an airplane is not to dive 300 feet underwater. A heavy rock is not to be used as a parachute. Gasoline is not to be used as a health drink. Marriage is not to be used for slavery. The church is not to be used as a _____. You fill in the blank. Authority is not to be used as a dictatorship that holds people in bondage. Yes, we have seen the abuse of authority but God always has and always will give humans authority to lead His people on earth.

The responsibility of leadership is to protect and train people to grow up and have freedom to do what they are called to do. Leadership is to bring order into the house which in turn produces peace in the house. Why do we need order in the house? Show me an eight-year old and a ten-year old home alone for more than an hour and I will show you chaos, power struggles and confusion. When dad walks in the room, governmental order walks in the room. It is the same with the body of Christ, the church is begging for order! Let me show you two ways confusion can come into a house.

Confusion

One way confusion comes into the house is when a person with no authority tries to lead. Human nature says I want to lead without going through the testing, training and proving. These people have no Godly authority, and are backed by no Godly power. Therefore they rely on an illegal power which uses intimidation, manipulation and domination to rule by. The Bible refers to it as witchcraft [I Sam. 15:23 KJV]. The Bible also likens these people as goats [Ezk. 34:17-21, Mat. 25:31-46]. If these goats are not confronted, an evil spirit called the "spirit of error" [I Jn. 4:6] is developed. If the "spirit of error" is not dealt with, it takes over and matures into a full blown "spirit of Jezebel" [I Kings 18,19,21, Rev. 2:20].

Another way confusion comes into the house is when people are given responsibility as leaders but given no authority to back their leadership. Or they are given authority but the boundaries or jurisdiction of their authority has not been defined for them and the people they lead. The "world" uses this system of ambiguity to control employees to nations. If you don't know what you are accountable for, who you are accountable to, and what the rules are, you can't play the game. Therefore you are subject to the whims of the "top leader." Good hard working "submissive to leadership people" are fired and "power hungry people" are promoted in this system.

In the world we expect that system to be working because the Bible tells us *"...Whose end is destruction, whose God is their belly, and whose glory is in their shame, who mind earthly things"* (Phil. 3:19). If that system flourishes in the Body of Christ it brings in *confusion*. May I belabor this point just a little further so you can see the practical side of this deception? I really want you to see how this world system of ambiguity has already infiltrated the church.

Exchanging Bible Words with Modern Words

In the "building" system we exchanged Bible words with modern words which became confusing. For example; The Church means people (the called out ones), but the "building" system turned the meaning into a nonprofit corporation that supported a building. The position of Elder was turned into a Board of Elders who were politically chosen and usually "yes" men. These men made financial decisions concerning the corporation.

In contrast, the Bible shows that the Eldership is a key position of the church, their qualifications are as spiritual leaders filled with the power of the Holy Spirit and able to pray the prayer of faith to save the sick (James 5:14)! Today in our ministry, we see Elders traveling to Deacon's homes, teaching and stirring up the younger in their Christian faith.

At one time communion, or The Lord's Supper, was a dinner that started with the breaking of bread in remembrance of Jesus, continued with a full meal, song, fellowship, prayer, the reading of scripture and ending with the drinking of the wine. This whole dinner was communion (1Cor. 11:20,21). The "building" system condensed it into a five minute ritual with juice and crackers.

What do we do with a Deacon? No one knows, so the "building" system turned that position into an usher, or it lets him run the "ministry of helps" (like a thrift store business). We went to the Bible to find out what a Deacon was in the early church. A Deacon was usually the one who opened his house and prepared the dinner for communion. He also had qualifications for his position (1 Tim. 3:8).

Next is the Bishop. (Isn't he the man with the three foot hat and long hanging robes in the movie "Princess Bride," and starts a wedding ceremony with a stuttering word; "M-OU-WAGE"?). No wonder the world makes fun of us, we are funny! The world laughs because we have been influenced by *them*! They should be influenced by us, do you not agree?

The God of Process

Truly our God is the God of process and we must believe we are in His perfect time. You may think you are a man or woman before your time. The truth is that you were birthed, born again, Spirit baptized, trained tested and retrained for such a time as this! Praise be to the Living God!

Few who look at a beautiful painting have an understanding of the painter's process. You might be viewing a painting of the seashore at sunset and marvel at its beauty and comment about the unique color and texture of the waves in the water. The artist just smiles and says thank you as he remembers the day he was painting it and his dog knocked over the canvas and stepped on that exact spot.

You see it is more about process than the end product. Once again, *it is more about process than the end product.* Why is it so hard to see what the church is supposed to look like in the Bible? It is difficult because what you are expecting isn't there.

So if you are looking for a formula or a perfect "paint by number picture" of the church, this following section will be greatly frustrating for you. Or worse, you might try to take the following example and make it fit into your previous system, then yell at God that it doesn't work, and tell me "I told you so." Oh well, mankind has been doing that for hundreds of years.

STOP!

PLEASE DON'T READ THIS SECTION!
UNTIL YOU HAVE READ ALL OF THE PREVIOUS
CHAPTERS.

Identifying the Church

In this section I will reveal to you what you have been searching for, but it has two parts. And if we have one with out the other, we have missed it altogether!

At this point most authors or speakers who are trying to reveal an error and present the revelation of truth would ask a favor. They would say I want you to hear this with an open mind. I say not on your life! I am asking that you don't have a closed or open mind. I'm telling you that it takes the mind of Christ [Phil. 2:5].

"For to us God revealed them through the Spirit; for the Spirit searches all things, even the depths of God. For who among men knows the thoughts of a man except the spirit of the man, which is in him? Even so the thoughts of God no one knows except the Spirit of God. Now we have received, not the spirit of the world, but the Spirit who is from God, that we might know the things freely given to us by God, which things we also speak, not in words taught by human wisdom, but in those taught by the Spirit, combining spiritual thoughts with spiritual words. But a natural man does not accept the things of the Spirit of God; for they are foolishness to him, and he cannot understand them, because they are spiritually appraised" (I Cor. 2:10-14).

Read the following prayer, and if you are in agreement with it, go back and pray it out loud!

Father God, Your word says in Phil. 2:5 that I can put on the mind and attitude of Christ, the Christos, the anointed one. You word says that the very mind of Christ can be in me. I proclaim, as Jesus is my Lord and Savior and His Holy Spirit dwells in me, that I also possess His very mind and attitudes. I proclaim this day that I have the mind of Christ! In Jesus' Name, Amen.

Did you pray it? If you did, then let's move ahead!

The Church and the Kingdom of God

Get the revelation that the church is people! So what does the church "look like?" People. People, people, people! *"He (Jesus) said to them, 'But who do you say that I am?' And Simon Peter answered and said, 'Thou art the Christ, the Son of the living God.' And Jesus answered and said to him, 'Blessed are you, Simon Barjona, because flesh and blood did not reveal this to you, but My Father who is in heaven.' 'And I also say to you that you are Peter, and upon this rock I will build My church; and the gates of Hades shall not overpower it'"* (Mat. 16:15-18).

Let's interpret the last half of verse 18 in the context of this chapter. Jesus simply said upon this rock. What rock? The one foundational rock that every believer has to enter with, stand on and allow to break us. The cornerstone of the church, the rock of the revelation that thou art Christ, the Son of the living God! Every one has to individually answer that question. So now let's interpret the whole thing.

Jesus simply said, upon the foundational revelation from the Father, that He (Jesus) is the Christ, the Son of the living God, would build His PEOPLE. He would build those that accept the call of coming out of a kingdom of darkness and into the kingdom of light, and a life of righteousness, peace and joy in the Holy Ghost. With the promise that; the many temptations, entrances or gates into hell shall not overcome them.

OK, is the understanding that the church is the "called out people" established in you, or do you need one more scripture? One more you say? Even Luke who wrote the book of Acts called Moses and his gang *"...the church in the wilderness..."* (Acts 7:38 KJV).

Now that we understand that Jesus is going to build His people, how is He going to do it? The very next verse Matt.16:19 gives us the "key" to the mystery. *"I will give you the keys of the kingdom of heaven..."* Jesus in the four gospels of his life is only recorded using the word *church* twice but uses the words; *the kingdom*, 125 times. So here in our quest of understanding what the church was, we were led to the next question, what is the kingdom? The church and the kingdom are different and if we have one without the other we have missed it all together.

The Kingdom of God—Not Denominations

It is as easy as this, if the church is the people then the kingdom is the structure, government, or authority, that holds the people together in unity and peace. The very word *denominations* is plural and means the division of nations, which is the exact opposite of kingdom. *"But, dear friends, remember what the apostles of our Lord Jesus Christ foretold. They said to you, 'In the last times there will be scoffers who will follow their own ungodly desires. These are the men who divide you, who follow mere natural instincts and do not have the Spirit"* (Jude 17-19).

Denominations divide the body of Christ with silly doctrines and traditions of men. Oh, there is some great organization in all denominations but it is all based on divisions. If you are sitting at home confused, hurt, isolated and unassembled, then you need to begin to pray for more understanding on how and where you and your family were derailed. Then get back on the RIGHT track! Maybe you need to go back and pray the prayer at the beginning of this section again? Go ahead, I'll wait. Seriously, pray it again.

Right on! Let's keep going. There is a large organization of "Christian" men that really hit the news media from 1995 through 1998 that promotes a false expectation of Denominational unity. They use this text *"...that all of them may be one, Father, just as you are in me and I am in you. May they also be in us so that the world may believe that you have sent me I have given them the glory that you gave me, that they may be one as we are one: I in them and you in me. May they be brought to complete unity to let the world know that you sent me and have loved them even as you have loved me"* (John 17:21-23).

Wow! That really sounds good and it can and will happen because *all* of Jesus' prayers are answered! But that scripture is not fulfilled when 60,000 men of 100 different denominations gather together in a big stadium. Why? Because they don't become one as Jesus and the Father are one.

If you have five different denominations gather together in a single service, you still have five separated groups in one building. But, you ask, *isn't that at least a start to unity?* Start to unity!? What unity? The Baptist have the secrete motive to get the Catholics in the room saved. The Nazarenes in their prayer meeting before the gathering are asking God to deliver the Assemblies of God people from that demon of speaking in tongues. And the Assemblies of God think they have the greatest revelations across the board so they get to lead the song service and show the rest of the groups how to "really worship." Then just wait until an offering is taken and the fight on which group gets the money. It is still five little separated kingdoms. Even some of the so-called independent ministries are a denomination, but they call themselves non-denominational. It is still a division.

It is at this very level of deception that the antichrist will come in and join all denominations under one flag. Every little divided-spiritual-kingdom joined together under the guise of peace and unity. One world order, one world government and one world "church."

The revelation to Daniel when he was interpreting the statue in King Nebuchadnezzar's dream was a little different. He said, *"...In the time of those kings, the God of heaven will set up a kingdom that will never be destroyed, nor will it be left to another people. It will crush all those kingdoms and bring them to an end, but it will itself endure forever"* (Dan. 2:44). Jesus said when you pray say *"Our*

Father in heaven...your kingdom come, your will be done on earth as it is in heaven" (Mat. 6:10).

Thy Kingdom Come

"This, then, is how you should pray: 'Our Father in heaven, hallowed be your name, your kingdom come, your will be done on earth as it is in heaven'" (Mat. 6:9,10). Who's kingdom come? Whose will be done? The kingdom belongs to the Father. Not to man, not to Satan, not to the angels—but to the Father. It is the Kingdom of God! Where is this kingdom and how do we get into it?

Kingdom of Darkness

The god of the kingdom of darkness is named Satan. He was seated in heaven in the very presence of God. But he was cast from heaven at the command of God, and awaits his final judgment. Among his many dark acts, he swindled the first lady and first man out of their title deed to this world. Because of their disobedience to God's command and believing a lie from Satan, sin entered the picture, which is separation from God. As we were birthed into this world through the first man Adam, that sin was passed down and we were born with a nature to sin. We were born in a separated condition apart from God. We were birthed into Satan's dark kingdom.

Kingdom simply means rule. *"We know that... the whole world is under the control of the evil one"* (I Jn. 5:19). *"...turn them from darkness to light, and from the power of Satan to God, so that they may receive forgiveness of sins and a place among those who are sanctified by faith in me"* (Acts 26:17,18). *"...if our gospel is veiled, it is veiled to those who are perishing. The god of this world/age has blinded the minds of unbelievers, so that they cannot see the light of the gospel of the glory of Christ, who is the image of God"* (2 Cor. 4:3,4).

The Good News

When we were born, we were given a deposit, if you will, deep down inside of us. That deposit is a pure question in our heart about our origin. Who am I? Where did I come from? What is my purpose? What happens to me after my body dies? When we become of the age when we begin asking these questions, we are driven to find answers. At that point the Holy Spirit of God brings books, tapes, songs, experiences, thoughts and people across our path to introduce us to a new kingdom.

We see someone a little happier than us, or one that is coping with life better than us and we ask them what is different with them. That person then begins to explain about the kingdom we live in and then compares it with the kingdom he lives in. *"And this gospel of the kingdom will be preached in the whole world"* (Mat. 24:14). *"For the kingdom of God ... is righteousness, peace and joy in the Holy Spirit"* (Rom. 14:17).

We then ask how to enter this kingdom. The answer is a matter of authority. We in the kingdom of darkness are under the authority of Satan, the authority he obtained when he swindled the title deed from the first man. God in turn bought back the title deed by paying the highest price for it. It cost the blood and death of God's Son Jesus. Then God resurrected Jesus from death, which entitled Jesus to not only rule in the Kingdom of God, but actually become the door into the kingdom Himself. He became the only door. *"Jesus answered, 'I am the way and the truth and the life. No one comes to the Father except through me'"* (Jn. 14:6). Again the answer is a matter of authority. *"That if you confess with your mouth, 'Jesus is Lord,'" and believe in your heart that God raised him from the dead, you will be saved"* (Rom. 10:9). You are saved out of the old kingdom of darkness and have entered into the new Kingdom of God through your confession of Jesus as your Lord.

Jesus spoke of this salvation as a new birth, *"...I tell you the truth, no one can enter the kingdom of God unless he is born of water and the Spirit. Flesh gives birth to flesh, but the Spirit gives birth to spirit"* (Jn. 3:5,6). In this new birth you become a member of God's kingdom and a member of God's household called the church!

Where is the Kingdom of God?

Where is the Kingdom of God? Wherever God is king! The kingdom of God is in heaven, but the kingdom of God is also on earth "in" you. *"The kingdom of God does not come with your careful observation, nor will people say, 'Here it is,' or 'There it is,' because the kingdom of God is within you"* (Lk. 17:20,21). *"...(God's) kingdom come, (God's) will be done on earth as it is in heaven."* (Mat. 6:9,10). *"But our citizenship is in heaven"* (Phil. 3:20). *"Therefore, if anyone is in Christ, he is a new creation; the old has gone, the new has come! ...gave us the ministry of reconciliation"* (2Cor. 5:17,18). *"We are therefore Christ's ambassadors, as though God were making his appeal through us..."* (2 Cor. 5:20).

The Kingdom of God is in heaven, and as you made Jesus the Lord of your life, the kingdom entered you. Now as a citizen of heaven, you have become an ambassador of Christ to this lost and dying world. You see you are still in this world but you are no longer of it! Your ministry is to reconcile people that are separated from God, back to God, by showing them the way to the kingdom door, Jesus! But you ask; "Is this a dangerous job?" Answer; it sure could be if you don't understand kingdom government.

Kingdom Government

Jesus established and mentored five distinct ministry styles in His work on this earth. Jesus the sent one...Jesus the proclaimer of truth...Jesus the preacher of the "good news"…Jesus the shepherd…and Jesus the teacher. He showed us five distinct areas of authority and the purpose of that authority. Then He ascended to His next place of ministry and authority, *"God has raised this Jesus to life, and we are all witnesses of the fact. Exalted to the right hand of God,"* *(Acts 2:32,33).* *"When he (Jesus) ascended on high, he (Jesus) …gave gifts to men"* *(Eph. 4:8).* *"It was he (Jesus) who gave some to be apostles, some to be prophets, some to be evangelists, and some to be pastors and teachers"* (Eph. 4:11). Why?

"…to prepare God's people for works of service, so that the body of Christ may be built up until we all reach unity in the faith and in the knowledge of the Son of God and become mature, attaining to the whole measure of the fullness of Christ. Then we will no longer be infants, tossed back and forth by the waves, and blown here and there by every wind of teaching and by the cunning and craftiness of men in their deceitful scheming. Instead, speaking the truth in love, we will in all things grow up into him who is the Head, that is, Christ" (Eph. 4:12-15).

Even though these five ministry gifts are not all accepted today, they are all in operation until Eph. 4:11-15 and this next scripture are completed. *"Husbands, love your wives, just as Christ loved the church and gave himself up for her to make her holy, cleansing her by the washing with water through the word, and to present her to himself as a radiant church, without stain or wrinkle or any other blemish, but holy and blameless"* (Eph. 5:25-27). The church isn't a bride without stain yet, therefore all five of these gifts are needed to complete the job.

Unfortunately, some of the people holding these ministry gifts of service perverted the authority entrusted to them, and turned their positions upside-down. They have manipulated the sheep (the body of Christ) to serve them (the shepherds). Let me show you a basic doctrine or principal throughout Scripture that today has largely become only lip-service; "to lead, is to serve" (Gal 5:13).

Jesus gave us the ultimate example of this "serving leader" principle recorded in John 13:3-17.

"Jesus knew that the Father had put all things under his power, and that he had come from God and was returning to God; so he got up from the meal, took off his outer clothing, and wrapped a towel around his waist. After that, he poured water into a basin and began to wash his disciples' feet, drying them with the towel that was wrapped around him. He came to Simon Peter, who said to him, 'Lord, are you going to wash my feet?' Jesus replied, 'You do not realize now what I am doing, but later you will understand.' 'No,' said Peter, 'you shall never wash my feet.' Jesus answered, 'Unless I wash you, you have no part with me.' 'Then, Lord,' Simon Peter replied, 'not just my feet but my hands and my head as well!' Jesus answered, 'A person who has had a bath needs only to wash his feet; his whole body is clean. And you are clean...'

"When he had finished washing their feet, he put on his clothes and returned to his place. 'Do you understand what I have done for you?' he asked them. 'You call me 'Teacher' and 'Lord,' and rightly so, for that is what I am. Now that I, your Lord and Teacher, have washed your feet, you also should wash one another's feet. I have set you an example that you should do as I have done for you. I tell you the truth, no servant is greater than his master, nor is a messenger greater than the one who sent him. Now that you know these things, you will be blessed if you do them.'"

Leadership from the Foundation Up

"Consequently, you are no longer foreigners and aliens, but fellow citizens with God's people and members of God's household, built on the foundation of the apostles and prophets, with Christ Jesus himself as the chief cornerstone. In him the whole building is joined together and rises to become a holy temple in the Lord. And in him you too are being built together to become a dwelling in which God lives by his Spirit" (Eph. 2:19-22).

Let's start the building with the cornerstone. Jesus, being the head of the church [Eph. 5:26] leads from the bottom up. He served the Father by giving His life, thus creating the foundational cornerstone. Everything else is measured and leveled from the cornerstone. Everything in the church must use Jesus as our "plumb line." If it doesn't measure up to Jesus, it can't be used in the church. The cornerstone is also the first stone in the dirt, and on the bottom so the rest of the structure may be built upon it. Let's look at the other foundational stones in the dirt.

Many denominations say that the church is built on the teaching of the apostles and prophets and once the Bible was written there was no need for theses gifts anymore. Is the foundation of God's household built on the teaching of the apostles and prophets, or on the very human gift that they are to the church? Are they living stones or not? Was Jesus given the position of the cornerstone for his teaching or was Jesus the cornerstone because of the sacrifice he made. We would have to say His sacrifice made him strong enough to be *THE* living stone.

"...now that you have tasted that the Lord is good. As you come to him, the living Stone—rejected by men but chosen by God and precious to him—you also, like living stones, are being built into a spiritual house to be a holy priesthood, offering spiritual sacrifices acceptable to God through Jesus Christ. For in Scripture it says: "See, I lay a stone in Zion, a chosen and precious cornerstone, and the one who trusts in him will never be put to shame. Now to you who believe, this stone is precious. But to those who do not believe, The stone the builders rejected has become the capstone, and, a stone that causes men to stumble and a rock that makes them fall. They stumble because they disobey the message" (I Pet. 2:3-8).

It is quite obvious that there are only twelve apostles of Jesus and twelve Fathers of the twelve tribes of Israel, which made up the twenty-four Elders around the throne. *"On the gates were written the names of the twelve tribes of Israel. The wall of the city had twelve foundations, and on them were the names of the twelve apostles of the Lamb"* (Rev. 21:12). But the New Testament list some nineteen other apostles by name, so clearly there were more, and are more, than the original twelve. The church is still being built upon the apostles and prophets. *"Now you are the body of Christ, and each one of you is a part of it. And in the church God has appointed first of all apostles, second prophets...* (I Co. 12:27,28).

The Five Governmental Gifts

Now that the cornerstone and the foundational stones are in place let's take a look at all five governmental gifts together. Still working from the ground up and all of the house "living stones." The apostle is first mentioned in the list and the name itself translates as an admiral in the navy, an ambassador of the Gospel, a commissioner of Christ, a sent one. Next is the prophet; a foreteller, a proclaimer of truth, a caller to purity and repentance. After these two come the evangelist, a preacher of the gospel, of the good news of the kingdom. Followed by the pastor, a leader, a feeder, a protector, a shepherd of sheep. Which brings us to the teacher, an instructor, a doctor, a master, and a keeper of doctrinal purity.

Elders and Deacons

Remember the church is the people and the Kingdom of God is the rule of God. Even though I present the government with pretty ridged guidelines, the key word is flexible! This is a body...the Body of Christ. Sometimes you don't have to use certain parts. For example, your body doesn't need to feel pain unless your hand is getting to close to a fire. When your hand IS getting to close to a fire, you need nerve endings that proclaim to your brain that the hand is in immediate danger.

In the same way some parts of the body of Christ might have a resident apostle, other parts might only have a relationship with an apostle and prophet that oversees from a distance. Likewise some parts of the body might have active elders and deacons, and other parts none. At any rate, elders and deacons do have character qualifications that must be met before serving in these offices, (ITim. 3). Governmental gifts have different authority and responsibility, but no gift is more valuable than the other. The goal is to understand where we fit in the body and get there!

In the prototype I am about to present, the elders and deacons fulfill a major role in ministry and discipling the many new believers

The Prototype

Everything I have put in this book came from this five-year prototype that I am about to show you. If you try to reproduce this model in a traditional, religious, building system, it will only become one of your many programs and it will die. On the other hand if you have never seen any other example except the building system, I believe you will be encouraged, and possibly get off your sofa and get back to what God has called you to.

This model of the church combined with the Kingdom of God has mostly been seen in third world countries where they can't afford the big building and the glamorous entertainment. They are literally forced to minister "house to house." In America or developed countries we have to choose to operate this way, and with what is just around the corner politically, we need to choose quickly.

The Wednesday Picture

It is Wednesday night and four to twelve people gather in a living room. Is it a Bible Study, a prayer meeting, a birthday party, a counseling session, a fundraiser, a share group, a deliverance night, a potluck or what? Yes, and more. It is the church. It is like a single cell of your body. It is where the very essence of life is. It is flexible, movable, mobil and alive! Everyone comes with the promise and expectation that "...where two or three come together in my name, there am I (Jesus) with them" (Matt. 18:20).

What makes this small group any different from any other small Christian group? And how do you "control" it so that it doesn't get into false doctrinal error and become a cult? Simple; there is kingdom government in the room.

First of all the owner of the home is there. The owner is the host, and if they have done their job well, the home is ready to greet the folks coming in. Then there is a deacon or deacon couple in the room, but a guest would never know it. Deacons just look like everyone else. Except they are a little sneaky when they walk into the kitchen and open the cabinets and fridge to make sure that host family has enough groceries for the week! What if there isn't enough food? It will be taken care of before the night is over. How? There is a deacon in the room! But it doesn't stop there, you would also find an elder or five-fold ministry gift that rotates into the group. They are a little easier to spot because they are apt to teach. They might even be the one to say "go" to start the meeting. If there is a rebuke in the room or if a demon is screaming out the door a pointed finger is probably coming from their direction. It is like dad being in the room.

It is safe to be yourself, to be intimate, transparent and encouraged to ask questions. A small group where you can learn to walk in the gifts of the Spirit, understand the depths of the Bible, and to sing out in worship! A place where relationships are born and nurtured. It is the Church in its smallest single cell. Outside of "one on one" discipleship these small groups are the most important, highly valued part of our ministry. These small groups don't get the leftovers, they get the maximum attention, resources and energy. They are the Church!

The Sunday Picture

Just about the same as Wednesday, except several of the small groups assemble together, as one large group. Where do we meet? Everyone puts a folding chair in their car and we travel house to house of course. On Wednesdays and Sundays we try to never meet in the same house two weeks in a row. We keep a pretty good rotation so that we don't offend any of our neighborhoods, or overuse any one home.

The "feeling" of the Sunday Celebration is one of a family reunion. We have no extravagant programs for children or youth. So the children might be outside playing in the yard or downstairs watching a video before the meeting actually gets rolling. Once most of the folks have arrived we say "go" and the children come into the middle of the living room and we begin to sing, testify, and worship the Lord with the freedom of the Gifts of the Spirit flowing. Once the meeting takes a path or the Holy Spirit begins to reveal a "flow" in a certain direction we simply follow it to the best of our ability.

Our children armed with coloring books, drawing paper and crayons go to the carpet and listen as the Word of God goes forth. Sometimes we have a couple of adults walk the children to a nearby park but we really like them to experience the flow of the Holy Spirit by staying in the meeting. There have been times when a child has looked up from her coloring, and came out with a prophetic word or prophetic answer to a question. The children are reminded that at anytime they see a picture, hear the voice of God, smell a unique smell, have an unusual pain or maybe even have a huge color in their mind, that they may tug on the leaders hand and share it. We encourage participation, with honor and respect, from everyone.

The prophet or prophetess may proclaim scripture along a certain line. The apostle may address a certain negative issue that has come up during the week or encourage those who have displayed a Godly character. The teacher may correct an error in teaching that has entered the camp. The evangelist may encourage the body to share their faith in Christ or show different ways to present the Kingdom of God to our world. The pastor may stand and have the elders come forward to anoint the sick with oil or have the deacons serve communion. As His church moves in His Kingdom the following scripture passage is fulfilled almost every time.

"But if an unbeliever or someone who does not understand comes in while everybody is prophesying, he will be convinced by all that he is a sinner and will be judged by all, and the secrets of his heart will be laid bare. So he will fall down and worship God, exclaiming, 'God is really among you!' What then shall we say, brothers? When you come together, everyone has a hymn, or a word of instruction, a revelation, a tongue or an interpretation. All of these must be done for the strengthening of the church. If anyone speaks in a tongue, two—or at the most three—should speak, one at a time, and someone must interpret. If there is no interpreter, the speaker should keep quiet in the church and speak to himself and God. Two or three prophets should speak, and the others should weigh carefully what is said. And if a revelation comes to someone who is sitting down, the first speaker should stop. For you can all prophesy in turn so that everyone may be instructed and encouraged. The spirits of prophets are subject to the control of prophets. For God is not a God of disorder but of peace. As in all the congregations of the saints" (I Co. 15:24-33).

Outside of an occasional all day Saturday School, Wednesday evenings and Sunday morning Celebrations are the only scheduled corporate meetings. What we find going on behind the scenes is families inviting guests over for dinner, sharing child care, or helping one another with a building or yard project, throughout the week. The relationships start turning into community! It does take time.

What About Growth?

Home meetings consist of about three to four families (around eight to sixteen people) with a Deacon or deacon couple to oversee organization. As the group grows and more deacons are raised up, one home meeting turns into two. About four to five home meetings (sixty to eighty people) make up a congregation. As the home meetings continue to reproduce, one congregation turns into two. We try to keep them as geographical as possible. The key word is still flexible. From time to time we might rent a hall or hotel room to have a ministry wide gathering but nothing can replace the intimacy of a home.

Remember these are people and families. If relationships are to develop, the groups have to be fairly centrally located. Young and old, married and single, all are in the same meetings and households. Remember the "feeling" is family reunion. How else can we fulfill this scripture?

"...be temperate, worthy of respect, self-controlled, and sound in faith, in love and in endurance. Likewise, teach the older women to be reverent in the way they live, not to be slanderers or addicted to much wine, but to teach what is good. Then they can train the younger women to love their husbands and children, to be self-controlled and pure, to be busy at home, to be kind, and to be subject to their husbands, so that no one will malign the word of God. Similarly, encourage the young men to be self-controlled. In everything set them an example by doing what is good" (Titus 2:2-7).

In every meeting from small to large we will always have three groups: children, young men and fathers (this is both spiritual and physical senses). *"I write to you, dear children, because your sins have been forgiven on account of his name. I write to you, fathers, because you have known him who is from the beginning. I write to you, young men, because you have overcome the evil one. I write to you, dear children, because you have known the Father. I write to you, fathers, because you have known him who is from the beginning. I write to you, young men, because you are strong, and the word of God lives in you, and you have overcome the evil one"* (I Jn. 2:12-14).

Discipleship, Training, Mentoring

For us, one of the greatest tools of understanding is that our growth *can* be measured. We can measure the growth of a tomato plant by the seed to the stalk, to the bud, to the small green fruit, to the ripened red fruit, to the taste of that first bite of the juicy matured-on-the-vine tomato! The same with the construction of a house, we can measure its growth. Plus in the process we have a "good" expectation that the growth will keep happening until the job is completed, step by step.

Unfortunately "the old religious system" has removed the growth stages from most discipleship so no one knows what the next step is, and then leadership becomes something mysterious and out of reach for the untrained. Why? Two reasons.

> 1. Leadership has gotten lazy and decided to bag the idea of Christian maturity, thus not having to be accountable to anyone.
> 2. Leadership wants to keep everyone babies so that no one will threaten their position of authority, and they can maintain a witchcraft control over the unlearned and immature.

But it is great to know that we can measure our spiritual growth from children to young men to adults! From ankle deep, to knee deep, to loin deep, to neck deep. From milk to meat. From carnal Christians, to Deacons, to Elders! Wow! The list goes on.

Unlike the Jews, American boys have a hard time with their manhood because they are confused when becoming a man. Jewish boys know from the beginning that they will be a man with responsibilities at the age of thirteen. American boys don't know if they become a man when puberty hits, or when they can vote, or go to war, or when they can legally drink hard liquor. Why? Because most of us have never established their training expectations, or qualifications.

Saints in the church need to know where they are now, what they are shooting for and how to get there. We need to know when we have completed a certain level, so we can look back and Praise God for the progress in our lives!! Each member needs to know where they fit in the body or they will be dysfunctional, and controlled by strong "leaders" with evil motives.

Discipleship at this time consists of an eleven week confrontational study. The new person follows a study guide that has about an hour a day fill-in-the-blank study, then at the end of the week this person meets with their sponsor. They take an hour to go over the study and apply the scripture to their lives. This course is geared to lay a foundation of the Kingdom of God and help the new person break strongholds.

Training involves all day Saturday schools on certain subjects. Different assignments to challenge the trainees on character issues, and opportunities to lead by serving. Books to read, tapes to listen to and people to minister to.

Mentoring is done as deacons model their lives to future deacons, elders to future elders and five fold gifts to future five fold. It is Moses and Joshua, Elijah and Elisha, and Paul and Timothy.

Deprogramming	Reprogramming
From—	To—
From doing (performance)	To Being
Programming and events	Relationships with God and body
Church is a building	Church is two or more people
Notebooks and lectures	Mentoring and modeling

Building an institution	Making disciples
Going to hear good sermons	Equipped for ministry
Few to use Spiritual Gifts	All using Spiritual Gifts
Most of resources on events	Majority of resources on people
Bring people for ministry	Go out to minister to people
Showing a form of Godliness	Accountable to walk in Godliness
System that uses/abuses people	Knowing and loving your brother

Government, Goals and Protocol

Host Homes
Opened by Disciples (possibly Deacons, Deacons in training, Elders or Five Fold).

Role of the Host:
"The end of all things is near. Therefore be clear minded and self-controlled so that you can pray. Above all, love each other deeply, because love covers over a multitude of sins. Offer hospitality to one another without grumbling" (I Pet. 4:7-9).

Expectations of the Host:
Open home for the Home Meeting to come to, get house physically clean (change kitty litter etc.) serve simple refreshment (ice

water with lemon). Invite a friend or neighbor. Pray and sing over the house to create an atmosphere condusive to the Presence of God. Participate in the meeting.

Qualifications of the Host:
- Born Again
- Started Discipleship Track #1.
- Knows the vision of the ministry.
- Able to receive instruction from a Deacon.

Protocol:
"Now we ask you, brothers, to respect those who work hard among you, who are over you in the Lord and who admonish you. Hold them in the highest regard in love because of their work. Live in peace with each other" (I Thes. 5:12,13).

"Do not rebuke an older man harshly, but exhort him as if he were your father. Treat younger men as brothers, older women as mothers, and younger women as sisters, with absolute purity. The elders who direct the affairs of the church well are worthy of double honor, especially those whose work is preaching and teaching. For the Scripture says, "Do not muzzle the ox while it is treading out the grain," and "The worker deserves his wages." Do not entertain an accusation against an elder unless it is brought by two or three witnesses. Those who sin are to be rebuked publicly, so that the others may take warning" (I Tim. 5:1, 2, 17-20).

Deacons
Home Meeting Leaders, (possibly Elders or Elders in training, or on hold Five Fold)

Role of Deacon:
"And we urge you, brothers, warn those who are idle, encourage the timid, help the weak, be patient with everyone. Make sure that nobody pays back wrong for wrong, but always try to be kind to each other and to everyone else. Be joyful always; pray continually; give thanks in all circumstances, for this is God's will for you in Christ Jesus. Do not put

out the Spirit's fire; do not treat prophecies with contempt. Test everything. Hold on to the good. Avoid every kind of evil" (I Thes. 5:14-22).

Expectations of Deacons:

Be a communication center. Organize meeting rotations, activate a prayer chain, love on the group (invite for dinner, send cards for birthday, anniversary, thinking of you). Be available for emergencies (partner fights, hospital visits). Know personal needs of group (food, transportation, health). Participate in weekly meetings, but use little rebuking, inform facilitating Elder of areas where help in the group is needed. Meets as a group with the Rotating Elders every two weeks.

Qualifications of Deacons:

Meet the same as the Hosts, plus:

• *"Brothers, choose seven men from among you who are known to be full of the Spirit and wisdom...a man full of faith and of the Holy Spirit...a man full of God's grace and power, did great wonders and miraculous signs among the people"* (Acts 6:3,5,8).

• *"Deacons, likewise, are to be men worthy of respect, sincere, not indulging in much wine, and not pursuing dishonest gain. They must keep hold of the deep truths of the faith with a clear conscience. They must first be tested; and then if there is nothing against them, let them serve as deacons. In the same way, their wives are to be women worthy of respect, not malicious talkers but temperate and trustworthy in everything. A deacon must be the husband of but one wife [at a time] and must manage his children and his household well. Those who have served well gain an excellent standing and great assurance in their faith in Christ Jesus. Although I hope to come to you soon, I am writing you these instructions so that, if I am delayed, you will know how people ought to conduct themselves in God's household, which is the church of the living God, the pillar and foundation of the truth"* (I Tim. 3:8-15).

• Must be publicly set in; *"They presented these men to the apostles, who prayed and laid their hands on them"* (Acts 6:6).

- Must tithe. *"Woe to you Pharisees, because you give God a tenth of your mint, rue and all other kinds of garden herbs, but you neglect justice and the love of God. You should have practiced the latter without leaving the former undone"* (Luke 11:42).
- Must have completed Discipleship Track #1

Protocol:
(Same as Hosts)

Elders

Rotating Facilitator (possibly Five Fold or Five Fold in training).

The Role of Elder:
"There is a time for everything, and a season for every activity under heaven" (Ecc. 3:1-8).
"...and the wise heart will know the proper time and procedure. For there is a proper time and procedure for every matter..." (Ecc. 8:5,6).

Expectations of Elders:
Facilitates Home Meeting with this charge; *"Preach the Word; be prepared in season and out of season; correct, rebuke and encourage— with great patience and careful instruction"* (II Tim. 4:2).
"...being the man of God thoroughly equipped for every good work...with and using God breathed Scripture..." (II Tim. 3:13).
Meets as a group with the Deacons every two weeks. Meets as a group with the Apostle at least once a month, as they help the Apostle with the steering of the overall ministry.

Qualifications of Elders:
Same as those of the Host and the Deacon, plus...
- *"Here is a trustworthy saying: If anyone sets his heart on being an overseer, he desires a noble task. Now the overseer must be above reproach, the husband of but one wife, temperate, self-controlled, respectable, hospitable, able to teach, not given to drunkenness, not violent but*

gentle, not quarrelsome, not a lover of money. He must manage his own family well and see that his children obey him with proper respect. (If anyone does not know how to manage his own family, how can he take care of God's church?) He must not be a recent convert, or he may become conceited and fall under the same judgment as the devil. He must also have a good reputation with outsiders, so that he will not fall into disgrace and into the devil's trap" (I Tim. 3:1-7)(Titus chapters 1, 2, 3).
- Must have completed Discipleship Track #2.
- Must practice the level of: *"I have been crucified with Christ and I no longer live, but Christ lives in me. The life I live in the body, I live by faith in the Son of God, who loved me and gave himself for me"* (Gal. 2:20).
- Must practice; *"All the believers were one in heart and mind. No one claimed that any of his possessions was his own, but they shared everything they had. With great power the apostles continued to testify to the resurrection of the Lord Jesus, and much grace was upon them all. There were no needy persons among them. For from time to time those who owned lands or houses sold them, brought the money from the sales and put it at the apostles' feet, and it was distributed to anyone as he had need"* (Acts 4:32-35).
- Must be able to discern the times and seasons Ecc. 3:1-8

Protocol
(Same as Hosts and Deacons.)

Body Working Together

As the skin, muscles, blood and bones of a human body overlap and blend together, supplying each part with protection, nourishment and communication, so the parts of the church overlap to do the same. Yet in the overlapping (of the human body or the church), it still maintains strict order.

"Just as each of us has one body with many members, and these members do not all have the same function, so in Christ we who are many form one body, and each member belongs to all the others. We have different gifts, according to the grace given us" (Romans 12:4-6).

Priorities of a Home Meeting

1. As the people come in the home, stir-up the mud or start collecting testimonies.

2. Lead the group into recognizing the presence of God in the room.

3. Activate the people to minister in the presence of God (or under an anointing or flow by the Spirit). Have them lay hands folks and pray or sing a Spiritual song.

4. Before you leave the meeting, look outside the group (outside themselves) and pray for lost friends and family, pray for evangelism strategies. Remind them that Jesus said "GO"!

Priorities of this Ministry

1. One-on-one discipleship. Mat. 18:19 ...if two agree...

2. House to House. Mat. 18:20 ...where two or three come together...

3. Discipleship Training School (DTS). Mat. 10:1-11:1 and Lk. 9:1-6 Special assignments to small groups.

4. Saturday Schools. Lk. 10:1-12 Special assignments to large groups.

5. Celebrations. Acts 2:1 ...all together in one place...

6. Networking. Mat. 14:21 ...Jesus feeds the 5000

Discipleship Track 1

Dates

_____ Enter a home group

_____ Received; "WELCOME TO CHANGED LIFE."

_____ Fill out "WELCOME TO CHANGED LIFE."

_____ Received "THE JOURNEY GUIDE."

_____ Filled out "THE JOURNEY GUIDE."

_____ Attend a New Believers Weekend

_____ Born Again. An understanding of;

_____ Jn. 3:3 _____ Jn. 3:16 _____ Romans 6:23 _____ Romans 10:9

_____ Acts 4:12 _____ Eph. 2:8,9

_____ Assurance of Salvation
_____ Read all of I Jn. _____ Jn. 3:36 _____ Jn. 5:24 _____ Jn. 17:3
_____ Prayer and Fasting Matt. 6:6
_____ Pray alone (Listening Room with a journal)
_____ Pray in the group with the laying on of hands.
_____ Matt. 6:17 But when you FAST,
_____ Water Baptism Matt. 3:11, Acts 10:47, Acts 2:38
_____ Assurance of Baptism Romans 6:3-5
_____ Baptism of Fire—Filled with Power of Holy Spirit Mat. 3:11
        Acts 1:8, Acts 2:2-4, Acts 10:38
_____ Speaks out in tongues 1 Cor. 14:2-5
_____ Prophesies
_____ Started Tithing Matt. 23:23

SERVE THE BODY Eph. 4:12
_____ Open your house to gather in.
_____ Help with the children.
_____ Send uplifting cards or phone calls.
_____ Matt. 6:3 "So when you GIVE,
_____ Bring in food for potluck or a need.
_____ Bring in finances for the ministry or a need.

STUDY- II Timothy 2:15
_____ Teamed with a Sponsor
_____ Started Arrival Kit - 11 sessions
_____ Finished Arrival Kit

OUTREACH- Mark 16:16-18
_____ Share your testimony with the group.
_____ Lead your children in salvation, baptism, prayer, and the power
        of the Spirit.
_____ Invite someone to come with you to a gathering.
_____ Visiting interested unbelievers.
_____ Share your testimony with someone outside the group.
_____ Sponsor person in Arrival Kit.
_____ Write and turn in your vision.

Video Tapes: 1 _____ 2 _____ 3 _____ 4 _____ 5 _____

Bible Reading:_____ Matthew _____ Mark _____ Luke _____ John
            _____ I Jn.

Get About God's Business

The individuals that have perverted their ministry gifts in the past are not our enemy. Put down your stones and get past them. They were called of God and will answer to God. If we yield to Satan and spend our time and energy fighting them, we have already lost the battle. When God confirmed to my wife and me to start this ministry, He spoke the same words to us individually and at the same time, but at different locations. I want to pass those same words along to you; Get about My business, saith the Lord!

Closing Thoughts

As you have read this book don't run off and tell your present leader or past leaders that they were wrong and then throw this book in their face. As you do start putting these principles into practice don't start preaching them to every religious person you know, or it will be like a herd of swine running over your valuable pearls. Most of all as you do begin to understand the freedom of this structure, don't try to just follow the structure by itself. You see without the Father's heart, everything you try will once again turn into religious bondage.

History has already proven that without an apostle or prophet, and the correct Kingdom government, the church is in complete disarray. If you don't know of an apostle or prophet, or are wondering about your own gifting, write me a letter. This is the "hour" for the church to grow up and all five ministry gifts are needed to get the job done.

This book and ministry are not about an organization, it is about Godly relationships in Godly order. Authority and leadership are not given or demanded out of an employee handbook or some denominational by-laws, but given and followed through those relationships that are in order. This life is about values. This walk is about value changes and breaking old religious habits such as performing for God and people instead of serving them.

If I have offended you I am truly sorry as that was neither my heart nor my intention. But obviously you too are questioning what the "Church" is all about, or you wouldn't be reading this book.

If you are a Pastor and this book has fallen into your hands, and sorrow or hopelessness has come upon you, write to me. Believe me I know how you feel. My livelihood came from that old system and when we stepped out, it was hard, very hard. But our God is faithful!

Over these last years we have a proven prototype that is alive and working. People are being born-again, filled with the power of God, delivered from strongholds, healed of diseases, restored in their marriages, discipled and trained for ministry, and new homes are being opened—thus the cycle continues.

At the time this book was written we are well into our third generation of disciples. May God grant us a Gideon's Army (Judges 7) and grant you a new vision of freedom.

For further information and additional copies of this book, please write to:

THE FAMILY CHURCH
PO Box 992, Enumclaw WA 98022

Individual orders—$7.95 per book
Bulk quantities (10 or more books)—$5.00 per book